PRACTICAL GUIDE OF
BIOPHARMACEUTICS
AND
PHARMACOKINETICS
FOR B PHARM STUDENTS

JASMINE KAUR RANDHAWA

© Jasmine Kaur Randhawa 2022

All rights reserved

All rights reserved by author. No part of this publication may be reproduced, stored in a retrieval system or transmitted in any form or by any means, electronic, mechanical, photocopying, recording or otherwise, without the prior permission of the author.

Although every precaution has been taken to verify the accuracy of the information contained herein, the author and publisher assume no responsibility for any errors or omissions. No liability is assumed for damages that may result from the use of information contained within.

First Published in April 2022

ISBN: 978-93-5611-288-9

Price: INR 200

BLUEROSE PUBLISHERS

www.bluerosepublishers.com
info@bluerosepublishers.com
+91 8882 898 898

Cover Design:
Muskan Sachdeva

Typographic Design:
Pooja Sharma

Distributed by: BlueRose, Amazon, Flipkart

Contents

1. To compute the pharmacokinetic parameter area under curve from given plasma concentration time data using numeric method. 1

2. To determine various PK parameters of drug following 1CBM(one compartment body model) kinetics after administration through IV infusion. 5

3. By using the given data 10

    (a) Determine wheather the decomposition follows Zero order kinetics or first order kinetics. 10

    (b) Also calculate the decomposition rate constant & half-life of drug in the body. 10

4. To calculate the elimination rate constant using urinary excreation data using rate of excreation and sigma minus method. 17

5. To verify the Noyes - Whitney law of dissolution. 22

6. To find the acid neutralization capacity of given brand of antacid tablets. 27

7. To perform the dissolution of tetracycline capsules and study the effect of antacid on its release 32

8. Apply method of residuals on the given data of drug obeying ICBM kinetics after administration as a single dose and also calculate various parameters using semilog graph paper 36

9. Apply method of residuals on the given plasma drug concentration – time data of a drug obeying 2CBM kinetics after IV bolus administration and calculate various PK parameters viz. intercept, microconstants and transfer rate constant using semi log graph paper 40

10. To compute various pharmacokinetic parameters from the given plasma drug concentration –time data of first order process using semilog graph paper and write down the equation for the line produced on the graph 47

11. To determine the absolute bioavailability and relative bioavailability from the given plasma concentration time data of the formulations containing the same drug 51

12. To compute various PK parameters using non-compartmental analysis from orally administered drug data 56

AIM No. 1

Aim: To compute the pharmacokinetic parameter area under curve from given plasma concentration time data using numeric method.

Reference: Lab manual of Biopharmaceutics and Pharmacokinetics by Dr. S.B.Bhise, Dr. R.J. Dias, Dr. S.C. Dhawale, Shri K.K.Mali ;Page No. 122-124

Requirements: Simple graph paper, Pencil, Scale, eraser, calculator, given pharmacokinetic data.

Theory: Area under curve represent the total integrated area under the plasma level time profile and express the total amount of drug that comes into contact of systemic circulation after the administration. Area under is expressed in mcg/ml x hours and is useful in estimating rate of absorption. Several methods are used for measuring the AUC like counting square, cutting and weighing method, using planimeter and trapezoidal rule method.

Trapezoidal rule method: It is simple numeric method of estimation of area under curve. In this method plasma concentration vs time data is plotted and the curve is divided by series of vertical lines into the trapezoids. The area of each trapezoid is calculated separately by using the following formula:

$$AUC = \frac{(C_{n-1} + C_n) \times (t_n - t_{n-1})}{2}$$

Where C is the concentration at given time t, t is the given time. The addition of area of all the trapezoids gives AUC. When the concentration at time zero is not indicated in data then for determination of AUC from conc. vs time obtained by following administration of drug orally, concentration at zero time is taken as zero. However when conc. vs time is plotted after IV administration, concentration at time zero is maximum hence it must be determined graphically in order to draw the first segment by trapezoidal rule. The advantage of this method is that it only require experimental data. The other methods involve greater numeric observations.

Procedure:

1. Take regular graph paper and plot given conc. vs time data by taking the time values on X-axis and conc. values on Y-axis.

2. Mark total number of segment (geometric trapezoids) on the graph paper and denote them with alphabets as A, B,C ……..etc.

3. Calculate the area of each segment using formula for geometric figure of segment.

$$AUC = \frac{(C_{n-1} + C_n) \times (t_n - t_{n-1})}{2}$$

4. The area bounded by trapezoid approximate area under curve.

5. Sum the area of all the segments to yield area under curve from time zero to time of last data plotted on the graph.

Example:

Given pharmacokinetic data: The plasma conc. after the administration of the single 500mg of drug dose orally is shown below. Calculate area under curve from zero to 5 hrs

Time (hrs)	0.5	1.0	1.5	2.0	2.5	3.0	3.5	4.0	4.5	5.0
Conc. (µg/ml)	1.5	16	35	45	32	20	14	10	8	5

Observation table:

Time (hrs)	Conc.(µg/ml)	Segment	$\frac{C_{n-1}+C_n}{2}$	$t_n - t_{n-1}$	AUC (µghr/ml)
0.5	1.5	A	0.75	0.5	0.375
1.0	16	B	8.75	0.5	4.37
1.5	35	C	25.5	0.5	12.7
2.0	45	D	40	0.5	20
2.5	32	E	38.5	0.5	19.25

3.0	20	F	26	0.5	13
3.5	14	G	17	0.5	8.5
4.0	10	H	12	0.5	6
4.5	8	I	9	0.5	4.5
5.0	5	J	1.5	0.5	3.25
					91.94

Calculations: Formula used:-

$$AUC = \frac{(C_{n-1} + C_n) \times (t_n - t_{n-1})}{2}$$

1. $AUC_{0-0.5} = \frac{1.5+0 \times (0.5-0)}{2} = 0.75 \times 0.5 = 0.375 \, \mu ghr/ml$

2. $AUC_{0.5-1.0} = \frac{1.5+16 \times (1.0-0.5)}{2} = 8.75 \times 0.5 = 4.375 \, \mu ghr/ml$

3. $AUC_{1.0-1.5} = \frac{35+16 \times (1.5-1.0)}{2} = 25.5 \times 0.5 = 12.75 \, \mu ghr/ml$

4. $AUC_{1.5-2.0} = \frac{45+35 \times (2-1.5)}{2} = 40 \times 0.5 = 20 \, \mu ghr/ml$

5. $AUC_{2-2.5} = \frac{32+45 \times (2.5-2.0)}{2} = 38.5 \times 0.5 = 19.25 \, \mu ghr/ml$

6. $AUC_{2.5-3.0} = \frac{20+32 \times (3.0-2.5)}{2} = 26 \times 0.5 = 13 \, \mu ghr/ml$

7. $AUC_{3-3.5} = \frac{14+20 \times (3.5-3.0)}{2} = 17 \times 0.5 = 8.5 \, \mu ghr/ml$

8. $AUC_{3.5-4} = \frac{10+14 \times (4.0-3.5)}{2} = 12 \times 0.5 = 6 \, \mu ghr/ml$

9. $AUC_{4-4.5} = \dfrac{8+10 \times (4.5-4)}{2} = 9 \times 0.5 = 4.5\ \mu g hr/ml$

10. $AUC_{4.5-5} = \dfrac{5+8 \times (5.0-4.5)}{2} = 6.5 \times 0.5 = 3.25\ \mu g hr/ml$

Result: The AUC from zero to 5 hrs is 91.94 μghr/ml

AIM No. 2

AIM: To determine various PK parameters of drug following 1CBM(one compartment body model) kinetics after administration through IV infusion.

References:

1. Laboratory manual of biopharmaceutics and pharmacokinetics by Dr S.B. Bhise, Dr.R.J.Dias, Dr. S.C. Dhawale & Shri K.K. Mali, Trinity publishing house, Page No. 119-121.

2. Biopharmaceutics and pharmacokinetics A traatise by D.M. Brahmankar & Sunil B. Jaiswal, Vallabh Prakashan Page No. 268-271.

Requirements: Semilog graph paper, regular graph paper, pencil, ruler, eraser, calculator, given pharmacokinetic data.

Theory: Rapid i.v. injection is unsuitable when the drug has potential to precipitate toxicity or when maintainance of a stable concentration in the body is desired. In such a situation, the drug like several antibiotics, theophylline etc is administered at a constant rate (zero order) by IV infusion instead of short duration of iv bolus (few seconds). The duration of constant rate infusion is usualy much longer than the half life of drug. This model is represented as:- →Elimination

Drug→ | Blood+ all other body tissue |

Zero-order

Infusion rate(R_o)

At any time during infusion, the rate of change in amount of drug in the body is the difference between the zero order rate of infusion R_o and first order elimination rate,-$K_E X$.

$$dX/dt = R_o - K_E X \quad \ldots\ldots\ldots (1)$$

Integrating the eqn. (1), we get

$$\int dX/dt = \int R_o - K_E X$$

$$X = \frac{R_o}{K_E}(1-e^{-K_E t}) \quad \ldots\ldots\ldots (2)$$

$$V_d C = \frac{R_o}{K_E}(1-e^{-K_E t})$$

$$C = \frac{R_o}{K_E V_d}(1-e^{-K_E t})$$

Put $Cl_T = K_E V_d$, $C = \frac{R_o}{Cl_T}(1-e^{-K_E t}) \quad \ldots\ldots\ldots (3)$

At the start of constant rate infusion, the amount of drug in the body is zero hence there is no elimination. As the time passes, the amount of drug in the body raises gradually(elimination rate less than the rate of infusion) until a point after which the rate of elimination is equal to the rate of infusion i.e. the conc. of drug in plasma approaches a constant value known as steady state platue conc. or at equilibrium the rate of change in amount of drug in the body is zero.

$$0 = R_o - K_E X_{ss}$$

$$K_E X_{ss} = R_o \quad \ldots\ldots\ldots (4)$$

Rearranging eqn. (4)

$$X_{ss} = \frac{R_o}{K_E}$$

$C_{ss} = \frac{R_o}{K_E} = R_o / Cl_T \quad \ldots\ldots (5)$ i.e. Infusion rate/clearance rate

$$K_E V_d$$

Where X_{ss} and C_{ss} are amount of drug in body and conc. of drug in plasma at steady state respectively.

Substituting eqn. (5) in eqn. (3), we will get eqn. (6)

$$C = C_{ss}(1-e^{-K_E t})\ldots\ldots(6)$$

Rearranging this eqn. yields

$$C = C_{ss} - C_{ss}e^{-K_E t}$$

Rearranging gives

$$C_{ss} - C / C_{ss} = - e^{-K_E t}\ldots\ldots(7)$$

Transforming eqn.(7) in log form we get

$$\log C_{ss} - C / C_{ss} = \frac{-K_E t}{2.303}\ldots\ldots(8)$$

Thus a semilog plot of $C_{ss} - C / C_{ss}$ vs t will result in a straight line with slope equal to $-K_E/2.303$ to reach steady state conc.

Example:

Given pharmacokinetic data: Estimate the vol. of distribution, elimination rate constant, half life & clearance from the given data obtained after infusion of drug at the rate of 50 mg/hr for 7.5 hrs.

Time(hrs)	0	2	4	6	7.5	9	12	15
Conc. (mg/lt)	0	3.4	5.4	6.5	7	4.6	2	0.9

Procedure: Given parameters:

$R_o = 50$ mg/hr

$C_{ss} = 7$ mg/lt which is conc. at steady state

1. Take a semilogrithmic graph paper & plot the graph between $C_{ss} - C/C_{ss}$ values on Y-axis & time values on X-axis as shown in observation table I upto steady state i.e. 7mg/lt conc. At 7.5 hrs. Also graph can be drawn on regular graph paper taking $\log C_{ss} - C/C_{ss}$ values on Y-axis & time values on X-axis as shown in observation table I upto steady state. A straight line with negative slope will be obtained in both graphs the slope of which can be calculated.

2. Mark the conc. values for respective time with pencil on the graph paper and draw a straight line through these points.

3. Determine the slope of the straight line using the following formula:

$$\text{Slope} = \frac{\log (C_{ss} - C/C_{ss})_2 - \log (C_{ss} - C/C_{ss})_1}{t_2 - t_1}$$

4. Calculate the elimination rate constant using formula

$K_E = -\text{slope} \times 2.303$

5. Calculate half life of drug using the formula:

$$t_{1/2} = \frac{0.693}{K_E}$$

6. Calculate the volume of distribution V_d using the formula:

$$V_d = \frac{R_o}{K_E V_d}$$

7. Calculate clearance by using the following formula:

$Cl_T = R_o / C_{ss}$

Calculations:

Observation table I

Time (hrs)	$\dfrac{C_{ss}-C}{C_{ss}}$	$\log \dfrac{C_{ss}-C}{C_{ss}}$
0	7 - 0 / 7 = 1	0
2	7 - 3.4/7 = 0.51	-0.292
4	7 - 5.4/7 = 0.228	-0.642
6	7 - 6.5/7 = 0.0714	-1.148

Slope by straight line of regular graph paper is as follows:

Slope = $\dfrac{-0.292-0}{2-0}$ = -0.146 mg/lt hr

Slope by straight line of semilog graph paper is as follows:

Slope = $\dfrac{\log 0.51 - \log 1}{2-0}$ = $\dfrac{-0.292-0}{2-0}$ = -0.146 mg/lt hr

(1) K_E = -(-0.146) x 2.303 = 0.336 mg/lt hr

(2) $t_{1/2}$ = 0.693/0.336 = 2.06 hrs

(3) V_d = $\dfrac{50}{7 \times 0.336}$ = 21.2 lts

(4) Cl_T = 0.336 x 21.2 = 7.12 lt/hrs

AIM NO. 3

Aim: By using the given data

(a) Determine wheather the decomposition follows Zero order kinetics or first order kinetics.

(b) Also calculate the decomposition rate constant & half-life of drug in the body.

References:

1. Lab manual of Biopharmaceutics & Pharmacokinetics by Dr. S.B. Bhise et al, Trinity Publication.

2. Biopharmaceutics and pharmacokinetics A treatise by D.M. Brahmankar & Sunil B. Jaiswal, Vallabh Prakashan Page No. 239-243.

Requirements: Pencil, eraser, calculator, regular graph paper, given data.

Theory: The velocity with which a reaction or process occurs is called the rate of reaction and the manner in which the conc. of drug influences the rate of reaction or process is called the order of reaction or order of process. Consider the following reaction:

$$A \rightarrow B \ldots \ldots (1)$$

Then the rate of forward reaction is expressed as:

Rate of forward reaction = $-dA/dt$ ……(2)

Negative sign in eqn. 2 indicate that the conc. of reactant A decreases with time. As the reaction proceeds, the conc. of product B increases with time and the rate of reaction is expressed as:

$$dB/dt \ldots \ldots (3)$$

Experimentally we can determine the rate of reaction by measuring the decrease in conc. of reactant A with time t. The rate of reaction is expressed as:

$dC/dt = -kC^n$ ......(4)

Where dC/dt is the rate of change in conc. of C with time t, K is rate constant; n is the order of reaction; C is the conc. of given species; n is order of reaction. If n=0, it is zero order process, if n=1, it is first order process.

Zero order kinetics: If n=0, the eqn. 4 becomes:

$$dC/dt = -K_0 C = -K_0 \ldots\ldots\ldots(5)$$

Where K_0 is zero order rate constant (mg/min), hence zero order process is defined as the one whose rate is independent of drug conc. Rearranging eqn. 5 gives:

$dC = -K_0 dt$ ......(6). Integrating eqn. (6) gives:

$$\int dC = -\int K_0 dt$$

$$C - C_0 = -K_0 t \ldots\ldots\ldots(7) \text{ or}$$

$$C = C_0 - K_0 t \ldots\ldots(8)$$

Where C_0 is conc. of drug at time zero; C is conc. of drug at time t. Eqn. (8) is that of straight line and states that conc. of reactant decreases linearily with time. A plot of C versus t yields a straight line having slope $-K_0$ and y-intercept C_0.

Zero-order half life: Half life is the time required for the conc. of drug to decrease by one-half. When $t = t_{1/2}$, $C = C_0/2$, the eqn. 8 becomes:

$$C_0/2 = C_0 - K_0 t_{1/2}, \text{ solving we get:}$$

$$t_{1/2} = C_0/2K_0 = 0.5 C_0/K_0 \ldots\ldots\ldots(9)$$

First order (linear kinetics):

If n=1, eqn. (4) becomes

$$dC/dt = -KC \ldots\ldots(10)$$

Where K = first order rate constant (in time^{-1})

Rearranging eqn. (10) gives:

$$dC/C = -Kt \ldots\ldots(11)$$

Integrating eqn. (11) gives:

$$\ln C = \ln C_0 - Kt \ldots\ldots(12).$$ Since $\ln = 2.303$ eqn. 12 becomes:

$$\log C = \log C_0 - \frac{Kt}{2.303} \ldots\ldots(12)$$

First order half life: Substituting the value of $C = C_0/2$, Eqn. 12 becomes $t_{1/2} = 0.693/K \ldots\ldots(13)$

(1) Equation method of finding order of reaction:

Put the given data into equations of zero order and first order kinetics and calculate the respective rate constants. Check that putting in which equation gives contant value of rate constant. The equation which gives constant value of rate constant, the rate follows that order of given reaction. See the solved example for reference.

(2) Graphical method of finding order of reaction:

Plot the given data of concentration vs time on regular graph paper taking conc. values on Y-axis and time values on X-axis. Check if the given plot is straight line, the given reaction follows zero-order kinetics. If the given plot is cartesian (regular), the reaction follows first order kinetics.

Given data:

Time(months)	Potency(%)
0	100
1	94.4
2	89.0
3	84
6	70.6
12	49.9
18	35.2
24	24.9
36	12.4

Calculations: (A) Equation method:

(I) Zero order kinetics is expressed by eqn.:

$C = C_0 - K_0 t$, putting the values of data into this eqn.:

1. $94.4 = 100 - K_0 \times 1$

$100 - 94.4 = K_0 = 5.6$

2. $89.0 = 100 - K_0 \times 2$

$100 - 89.0 = 2K_0$

$K_0 = 5.5$

3. $84.0 = 100 - K_0 \times 3$

$100 - 84.0 = K_0 \times 3$

$K_0 = 5.3$

4. $70.6 = 100 - K_0 \times 6$

$100 - 70.6/6 = K_0 = 4.9$

5. $49.9 = 100 - K_0 \times 12$

$100 - 49.9/12 = K_0 = 4.1$

6. $35.2 = 100 - K_0 \times 18$

$100 - 35.2/18 = K_0 = 3.6$

7. $24.9 = 100 - K_0 \times 24$

$100 - 24.9/24 = K_0 = 3.1$

8. $12.4 = 100 - K_0 \times 36$

$100 - 12.4/36 = K_0 = 2.4$

(II) First order kinetics is expressed by following eqn.

$$\log C = \log C_0 - \frac{Kt}{2.303}$$

1. $\log 94.4 = \log 100 - Kt/2.303$

$0.987 = 2 - K \times 1/2.303$

K=0.06 months^{-1}

2. log 89.0=2-Kx2/2.303

1.949=2-2K/2.303

K=0.058 months^{-1}

3. log 84.0=2-Kx3/2.303

1.92=2-3K/2.303

K=0.06 months^{-1}

4. log 70.6=2-Kx6/2.303

1.848=2-6K/2.303

K=0.058 months^{-1}

5. log49.9=2-Kx12/2.303

1.698=2-12K/2.303

K=0.057 months^{-1}

6. log 35.2=2-Kx18/2.303

1.546=2-18K/2.303

K=0.058 months^{-1}

7. log 24.9=2-Kx24/2.303

1.396=2-24K/2.303

K=0.058 months^{-1}

8. log 12.4=2-36K/2.303

1.093=2-36K/2.303

K=0.058 months^{-1}

The above calculations show that the rate constant is constant with eqn. of first order kinetics, hence the decomposition follows first-order kinetics

(B) Graphical method: Plot graph of conc. vs time, it results in cartesian curve, hence the given decomposition follows first order kinetics.

Decomposition rate constant = 0.06 months^{-1}

Half-life = 0.693/0.06 = 11.55 months.

AIM No.4

Aim: To calculate the elimination rate constant using urinary excreation data using rate of excreation and sigma minus method.

References:

1. Biopharmaceutics & Pharmacokinetics A treatise by D.M. Brahmankar and Sunil B. Jaiswal, Page No.285-289.

2. Biopharmaceutics & Pharmacokinetics (Theoretical concept &Illustrative practical exercise by Dr. Javed Ali et al.

Requirements: Semilog graph paper, calculator, scale, pencil, eraser & given pharmacokinetic data.

Theory:

Determination of K_E from urinary excreation data:

The first order elimination rate constants can be computed from urine data by two methods:

1. Rate of excreation data
2. Sigma minus method

Rate of excreation data: The rate of urinary drug excreation dXu/dt is directly propotional to the amount of drug in the body X and written as:

$$dXu/dt = K_e X \quad \ldots\ldots(1)$$

Where K_e=first order urinary excreation rate constant. As according to first-order disposition kinetics,

$$X = X_0 e^{-K_E t} \quad \ldots\ldots(2)$$

Substituting for the value of X in the value of X in the eqn.1, we get:

$$dXu/dt = K_e X_0 e^{-K_E t} \quad \ldots\ldots(3)$$

Where X_0=dose administration (i.v. bolus)

Upon transformation to log form, the eqn. becomes:

$$\log dXu/dt = \log K_eX_0 - \frac{K_Et}{2.303} \quad \ldots\ldots\ldots(4)$$

The above eqn. States that a semilog plot of rate of excreation versus time yields a straight line with slope $-K_E/2.303$. It must therefore be remembered that the slope of an excreation rate vs time plot is related to the elimination rate constant K_E and not to the excretion rate constant K_e. The K_e can be obtained from the y-intercept($\log K_eX_0$). Elimination half life and non renal elimination rate constant can be computed from K_E and K_e. An advantage is that for drugs having long half lives, urine may be collected for only 3-4 half-lives. Also, there is no need to collect all urine samples since collection of any two consecutive urine samples yield points on the rate plot from which a straight line can be obtained.

Sigma minus method: A disadvantage of rate of excreation method in estimating K_E is that fluctuations in the rate of elimination are observed to a high degree and in most instances the data are so scattered that an estimate of half life is difficult. These problems can be minimized by using alternative approach called as sigma minus method.

From the eqn.3 :

$$dXu/dt = K_eX_0e^{-K_Et}$$

Integrating above eqn. Yields:

$$Xu = K_eX_0(1-e^{-K_Et}) \ldots\ldots(5)$$

Where Xu=cumulative amount of drug excreated unchanged in urine at any time t. As time approaches infinity i.e. after 6-7 half lives, the value of $e^{-K_E\infty}$ becomes zero and therefore the cumulative amount excreated at infinite time $Xu\infty$ can be given by the eqn.

$Xu_\infty = K_e X_0 / K_E$ ……. (6)

Substituting eqn. 6 in eqn. 5 and rearranging it yields:

$Xu_\infty - Xu = Xu_\infty e^{-K_E t}$ ……… (7)

Converting to logarithms, we get

$$\log(Xu_\infty - Xu) = \log Xu_\infty - \frac{K_E t}{2.303} \quad ……..(8)$$

Where $Xu_\infty - Xu$ = amount remaining to be excreated i.e. ARE at any given time. A semi log plot of ARE versus t yields a straight line with slope $-K_E/2.303$. This method is known as ARE plot method. A disadvantage of this method is that total urine collection has to be carried out until no unchanged drug can be detected in the urine i.e. upto 7 half-lives, which may be tedious for drugs having long $t_{1/2}$.

Procedure: Using the following urinary excretion data, find the elimination rate constant using rate of excretion method and sigma minus method.

Data:- A single IV dose of an antibiotic was given to a 50 kg woman at a dose of 20 mg/kg. Urine samples were removed periodically and assayed for the parent drug. The following data were obtained (50x20=1000mg dose)

Time(hr)	dXu(mg)
0.25	160
0.50	140
1.0	200
2.0	250
4.0	188
6.0	46

Procedure: Rate of excreation method:

1. Take a semilogarithmic graph paper and plot a graph between dXu/dt and t* (mid-point time of urine collection).

2. The slope of the line obtained is equal to $K_E/2.303$ where K_E is elimination rate constant.

3. Calculate the elimination $t_{1/2}$ using the following equation:

$$t_{1/2} = 0.693/ K_E \ldots\ldots(9)$$

4. The urinary excreation rate constant(Ke) can be calculated from the intercept on y-axis where intercept is equal to KeX_0 where X_0 is the dose administered(1000mg).

5. The extra-renal excretion rate constant can be calculated using the equation:

$$K_m = K_E - Ke \ldots\ldots(10)$$

Sigma minus plot method: Using the same urinary excreation data, calculate the elimination rate constant using sigma minus plot method.

Reason: The disadvantage with the rate of excreation method for calculating K_E is that fluctuations in the rate of drug elimination are observed to a high degree and in most instances, data are so scattered that an estimate of half life is difficult.

Procedure:

1) Take a semilogarithmic graph paper and plot a graph between $Du_\infty - Du$ versus mid point of urine collection period which yields a straight line graph.

2) The slope of the straight line obtained gives the value of elimination rate constant as the slope is equal to $-K_E/2.303$.

3) Calculate the elimination half life ($t_{1/2}$) using the equation:

$$t_{1/2} = 0.693/K_E \ldots\ldots(9)$$

Observation Table for Rate of excreation method:

Time(hrs)	Mid point of urine collection (t*)	Time interval (dt) for urine collection	dD_u(mg)	Excreation rate dDu/dt(mg/hr)
0.25	0.125	0.25	160	160/0.25= 640
0.5	0.375	0.25	140	140/0.25 = 560
1	0.750	0.5	200	200/0.5 = 400
2	0.150	1	250	250/1 = 250
4	3	2	188	188/2 = 94
6	5	2	46	46/2 = 23

Observation table for Sigma-minus method:

Time(hr)	D_u (mg)	Mid point of urine collection time (t*)	Cumulative D_u (mg)	$D_U^\infty - Du$ (mg)
0.25	160	0.125	160	984-160 =824
0.50	140	0.375	300	984-300 = 684
1.0	200	0.750	500	984-500 = 484
2.0	250	0.150	750	984-750 = 234
4.0	188	3	938	984-938 = 46
6.0	46	5	984 = D_u^∞	984-984 = 0

AIM NO. 5

AIM : To verify the Noyes - Whitney law of dissolution.

References:

1. Biopharmaceutics & pharmacokinetics(Theoretical concepts & Illustrative practical exercises) by Dr. Javed Ali, Dr. Alka Ahuja, Dr. Sanjula Baboota and Dr. R.K.Khar, Page No. 306-309.

2. Biopharmaceutics and pharmacokinetics (A Treatise) by D.M. Brahmankar and Sunil B. Jaiswal, Page No. 29-33.

Requirements: Conical flask, glass rod, test-tube, test tube stand, blade, vernier calliper, ruler, hot plate, Nessler's cylinder, burette, burette stand, volumetric flask(100ml),conical funnel, filter paper.

Chemicals Required: Benzoic acid, soft paraffin, sodium hydroxide, distilled or purified water, phenolphthalein indicator, oxalic acid, ice.

Theory: Dissolution is a process in which a solid substance solubilises in a given solvent i.e. mass transfer from the solid surface to the liquid phase. The rate of dissolution of a solute particle depends upon the surface area of the solid which in turn depends upon how finely the drug is subdivided. It also depends upon energy and energy states within the crystals of drug. The Noyes-Whitney eqn. incorporates the major factors involved in the rate of dissolution i.e.

$$dC/dt = K.S.(C_s - C) \quad \ldots\ldots(1)$$

Where dC/dt = dissolution rate of the drug particles

K= dissolution rate constant (first order)

C_s = concentration of drug in the stagnant layer i.e. concentration at the saturation.

C= concentration of a drug in the bulk of solution at any given time t.

C_s -C represent the conc. gradient between the diffusion layer and bulk solution

Further in dissolution rate limited absorption, C will always be negligible as compared to C_s hence it can be neglected and the eqn. reduces to:

$$dC/dt = \frac{D \cdot S \cdot C_s}{H} \quad \ldots\ldots(2)$$

From this equation, it is clear that the rate of dissolution (dC/dt) is proportional to the surface area, S, of the solid and the concentration gradient. The dissolution rate K is unique to the chemical substance and incorporates energy and entropy factors. It varies widely from drug to drug and some drugs may have a slow rate of dissolution even despite a fine state of subdivision eg. Some preparations of aluminium hydroxide completely dissolve in gastric juice within 30 minutes while others no appreciable dissolution within 1 hour. Some drugs may exist in more than one crystal form so that there may be more than one K.

Noyes-Whitney eqn. assumes that the rate of mass transfer depends on the rate at which the solute diffuses from the thin boundary layer into the bulk solution.

Therefore K will depend on the diffusion coefficient of the solute and the thickness of the diffusion pathway and it will be influenced by factors that influence the diffusion coefficient and the film thickness.

If the surface area is kept constant, then

$K/S = K \ldots\ldots (3)$

$K \cdot S = K' \ldots\ldots (4)$

Therefore, eqn. (4) reduces to

$dC/dt = K'(C_s - C)$

$2.303 \log C_s/C_s - C = K't$

Dissolution rate for a particular drug in a particular solvent can be calculated as:

$K' = K/S$

Procedure:- Preparation of benzoic acid sticks

1. Weigh about 100 mg of pure benzoic acid crystals into a conical flask and melt on a hot plate. (Heating should not be so vigorous so that benzoic acid gets dissolved).

2. Take a glass rod and a test-tube

3. Flatten the one end of the glass rod so that to fit into the test-tube and place this test-tube on a test tube stand.

4. Hold glass rod in the center of the test tube and pour molten benzoic acid carefully. Fill it upto 9-10 cm height. Hold the rod in the center till benzoic acid begins to solidify.

5. Allow it to cool to room temperature and then place it in ice-bath for 10-15 minutes. (Due to further cooling benzoic acid will shrink and dislodge from surface of the test-tube. After thorough cooling ,pull out the glass rod along with the benzoic acid cylinder.

6. Cut with a blade to a length of 6-8 cm. Measure the exact length with scale and also the diameter with the help of vernier callipers.

7. Smear some soft paraffin on two opposite surfaces of stick (cylinder). This is done to prevent the surfaces from the dissolution. Excess of soft paraffin should be avoided as it would then diffuse to the benzoic acid stick and will spoil the circular surface.

8. Fill a pair of Nessler's cylinder upto 100 ml with distilled water. Two sticks of measured diameter were put in the pair of Nessler's cylinder(one in each cylinder) and move it up and down for 10 minutes.(During these 10 minutes, solid surface of benzoic acid sticks comes in contact with solvent.

9. The benzoic acid dissolved can be determined easily by titrating with standardized 0.05 N NaOH solution.

10. Weigh about 2 gm of sodium hydroxide into a 1000ml volumetric flask and make up the volume upto the mark with purified water to prepare the strength 0.05N NaOH solution.

Standardization: Prepare 0.025M oxalic acid solution and transfer into clean burette. Pipette 10 ml of prepared NaOH solution into a conical flask, add 1-2 drops of phenolphthalein indicator and titrate with the oxalic acid until end point is attained. Repeat the titration in triplicate until determinations agree with 0.05 ml of each other. Record the volume consumed of oxalic acid in the observation table and calculate the molarity of NaOH solution by following formula:

Molarity of NaOH = $\dfrac{0.025 \times \text{Volume consumed of oxalic acid}}{10}$

11. Withdraw about 10ml of the solution into a conical flask and titrate with standardized 0.05N NaOH using phenolphthalein as an indicator.

12. Similarly, withdraw the samples after 20,30 and 40 minutes and determine the concentration of benzoic acid (i.e. C_{20}, C_{30} and C_{40}) in the respective samples.

13. Prepare a saturated solution of benzoic acid in water by adding 200mg of benzoic acid in 50 ml of water, agitate and filter. Withdraw 10 ml of this saturated solution and determine the quantity of benzoic acid by titrating with standardized 0.05N NaOH (This gives the value of C_S) solution.

14. Plot the graph between log C_S/C_S-C vs time to get straight line, the slope of which gives K = slope x 2.303.

Observations:

Time (minutes)	C (concentration at time t)(mg/ml)	C_S/C_S-C	log C_S/C_S-C
0			
10			
20			
30			
40			

Hence Noyes Whitney eqn. is verified.

AIM NO.6

To find the acid neutralization capacity of given brand of antacid tablets.

Reference: Biopharmaceutics & pharmacokinetics (Theoretical concepts & illustrative exercises) by Dr. Javed Ali, Dr. Alka Ahuja, Dr.Sanjula Baboota, Dr. Roop K.khar, Birla publications Pvt. Ltd ,Page no. 299-303

Requirements: magnetic stirrer, pH meter, 100ml beaker, volumetric flask (100ml), given antacid tablets, Hydrochloric acid, sodium hydroxide, pestle & mortar, burette, conical flask, phenolphthalein indicator, measuring cylinder

Theory: Antacids are alkaline bases used to neutralize the excess gastric hydrochloric acid associated with gastric ulcers and hyperchlorhydria. An antacid should possess the following properties.:

1 It should not be absorbable or cause systemic alkalosis.

2 It should not be absorbable laxative or constipative

3 It should exert its effect rapidly and over longer period of time.

4 It should buffer in the pH 4-6 range.

5 It should probably inhibit pepsin

6 The reaction of the antacid with gastric HCl acid should not cause a large evolution of gas.

Antacids which are commonly employed are:

1 Aluminium hydroxide gel

2 Almina and Magnesia oral suspensions

3 Bismuth subnitrate

4 Bismuth subcarbonate

5 calcium carbonate,precipitated

6 Cholestryramine resin

7 Dihydoxylaluminium aminoacetate

8 Dihydroxylaluminium sodium carbonate

9 Magaltrate

10 Magnesium carbonate

11 Magnesium hydroxide

12 Magnesium trisilicate

13 Sodium bicarbonate

Three factors have an important bearing on the effectiveness of antacid therapy:-

1 Acid neutralization capacity of the antacid

2 Treatment schedule:- Antacids are commonly prescribed one hour after each meal and at bedtime

3 Patient compliance:- If an antacid provides unpleasant side effects and if the preparation employed lacks palatability ,poor patient compliance should be expected

Antacids do relieve the pain of peptic ulcer, are relatively free of side effects when properly used and do not prolong the ulcers. Since the actual mechanism for their relieving of pain is not known, the evaluation of antacids is difficult. While some evaluations are based on the subjective measurement of pain reduction, most are based on the effect of modifying the stomach pH. Although the latter approach would appear to involve a simple procedure, it is difficult to determine wheather the comparative in –vitro results have any clinical significance. Many in vitro techniques have been published. The range from adding the antacid to a given amount of hydrochloric acid and measuring the amount of antacid consumed in attempt at mimicking what goes on in the stomach. In acid to do the latter , an additional antacid is added at given time intervals in order to mimic the continuing secreation of acid into the stomach.

The in vivo evaluation of antacids is more difficult as it involves either removing aliquots of the gastric contents at intervals and measuring pH with electrodes in the stomach. The latter can be accomplished by using miniaturized pH meter which the subject swallows usually as a capsule. It can be held in a certain location and later recovered by attaching a string to it prior to swallowing the meter. The pH changes along the persons GIT can also be followed by simply allowing the meter to be carried along by peristaltic movement. X-rays give the exact location of the pH meter at any given time. The pH readings are usually transmitted by a radio signal.

Important factors which influence the clinical selection of antacid are:-

1 The antacids vary markedly in their in-vivo and in-vitro potency. This suggests that it is preferable to judge antacid dosage according to milli-equivalents of neutralizing capacity rather than volume of liquid or number of tablets. Other factors which should be considered include cost, taste, salt content, bowel habit ,underlying disease other than peptic ulcer and side effect.

2 Individual patient response to an antacid varies widely and cannot be predicted from measurements of acid secretion. Thus some patients have a marked reduction in gastric acidity after small doses of antacids whereas others have a poor response after larger doses.

3 The commomly recommended doses of antacid for treatment of duodenal ulcers are too low. Most physicians use 15 ml (1 tablespoonful) regardless of the antacids prescribed. Since antacid buffering stimulates gastric acid secretion the dose should be large enough to neutralize maximum acid secreation.

Acid neutralization capacity test:- This test is mentioned in the code of federal regulations that form a part of FDA regulations for ensuring that OTC antacid products shall be recognized as safe and effective and they shall not be misbranded. This test is general in nature and while it is obligatory that OTC antacid products comply with the requirements of safety and application for the purpose of determining the strength, quality and purity of official antacid, the pharmacopoeial standards and tests are generally specified in individual monographs which are required to be carried out.

Procedure:

Preliminary antacid test:- This test consists of:-

1. pH meter:-Standardize the pH meter at pH 4.0 with a standard buffer and check for a proper operation at pH 1.0 with 0.1 HCl.
2. Preparation of 0.1N HCl :- Dilute about 0.8 ml of concentrated hydrochloric acid to 100ml with distilled water in a 100ml volumetric flask.
3. Dosage form testing:-

a) Liquid sample:- place an accurately weighed and well mixed amount of antacid product equivalent to minimal labeled dosage (i.e.5ml) into a 100ml beaker. Add significant water to produce final volume to 40 ml. Mix with the magnetic stirrer at 300±30rpm for 1 minute. Then analyze the sample according to the following procedure:-

1 Add about 10 ml of 0.5 N HCl to the test solution while stirring on a magnetic stirrer at 300±30rpm.

2 Continue stirring for about 10 minutes after the addition of acid

3 Then note the pH of the solution.

4 If the pH value obtained is below 3.5, the product shall not be a labeled antacid.

5 If the pH is 3.5 and above, determine the acid neutralizing capacity as described in the ANC test.

b) For chewable and non-chewable tablet samples: Crush the tablets and accurately weigh an amount of sample equivalent to minimal labeled dosage into a 100ml beaker after passing through a sieve. Mix the sieved material to obtain uniform material. If wetting is needed, add not more than 5ml of 95 %alcohol. Mix to wet the sample thoroughly. (More amount of alcohol can affect the neutralizing capacity).Add sufficient water to produce the final volume to 40ml. Mix on a magnetic stirrer at 300±30rpm for 1 minute and analyze the sample according to the procedure described under liquid sample.

c) Effervescent sample:-Place an amount equivalent to minimal labeled dosage into a 100ml beaker. Add 10 ml of water and swirl the beaker gently while allowing the reaction to subside. Add another 10ml of water and swirl the beaker gently. Wash down the walls with 20ml of water. Mix with a magnetic stirrer at 300±30rpm for 1 minute and analyze according to the procedure described under liquid sample.

Acid neutralizing capacity test (ANC test):-

1 Preparation of 0.05N HCl :-Dilute about 4.5 ml of concentrated hydrochloric acid upto 1000ml with distilled water to prepare 0.05N HCl

2 ANC test:- Take one dose of an antacid and add 200ml of 0.05N HCl .Stir and note the pH at the end of 10,15 and 20 minutes. At the end of 20 minutes, the pH should not be less than 3.5 and not more than 4.2. Stir and add 10ml of 0.05N HCl .Continue stirring and titrate with 0.1N NaOH to a pH 3.5.The antacid passes the test if not more than 35ml of NaOH is used for titration.

Calculate the number of mEq of acid neutralized by the sample:

Total mEq= (30ml) X (Normality of HCl)- (ml of NaOH)(Normality of NaOH)

Calculations:

Batch	No. of mEq of acid neutralized by sample=(30x Normality of HCl)-(volume of NaOH used) (Normality of NaOH)
Batch I	
Batch II	
Batch III	

Result: The given sample of antacid passes/fail the test. The number of mEq of acid neutralized by the sample are: -

AIM NO: 7

To perform the dissolution of tetracycline capsules and study the effect of antacid on its release

References: 1) Effect of antacids on the dissolution behaviour of tetracycline and methacycline by Shozo Miyazaki, Hitoni Inone and Tanekazee, Faculty of pharmaceutical sciences, Josai university

2) Effect of antacids on the dissolution behavior of Methacycline and Doxycycline by Nazma Sultana et al, Journal of Pakistan Medical association, page 59-63

3) "Tetracycline Hydrochloride capsules", The united states pharmacopeial convention, 2010

Requirements: Dissolution apparatus, test tubes, test tube stand, conical funnel, filter paper, weighing balance, beakers, UV-spectrophotometer, given tetracycline capsules, given antacid powder, sieves(170 mesh), distilled water

Theory: Tetracyclines are a broad spectrum polypeptide antibiotics produced by the streptomyces genus of Actinobacteria and used against many bacterial infections. It is a protein synthesis inhibitor. The tetracyclines contain four rings in their structure. Tetracyclines have a broad spectrum of antibiotic action. The tetracyclines are incompletely and irregularly absorbed from the gastrointestinal tract. Absorption is most active in the stomach and upper small intestine and is greater in the fasting state. It is much less complete from the lower portions of the intestinal tract and is negligible from the colon. It is well known fact that antacids containing divalent or trivalent cations such as Calcium ion, magnesium ion or aluminium ion depress the absorption of orally administered tetracycline. Chelation is generally considered to be the mechanism responsible for the decreased absorption of tetracycline in the presence of antacids. Other antacids without divalent or trivalent cations may also affect the dissolution of tetracycline.

Procedure:

1 Transfer an accurately measured 900ml of purified water (USP official dissolution medium) into the dissolution vessels of the dissolution apparatus (USP, paddle Type II)

2 Take the given antacid powder and pass through a 170 mesh sieve.(The given antacid can be magnesium trisilicate, synthetic aluminium silicate, aluminium magnesium silicate bismuth)

3 Weigh about 1.8 gm of the given antacid powder.(0.2% w/v)

4 Pour the given antacid tetracycline Hydrochloride capsules in the dissolution vessels of the dissolution apparatus. Add the weighed antacid powder to one of the vessel.

5 Run the dissolution at $37^{\circ}C$ for 60 minutes(90 minutes for 500 mg capsules) at 75 rpm maintaining a distance of 45±5 mm between the blade and inside bottom of the vessel.

6 Withdraw about 5ml of the sample from each vessel periodically with the interval of 5 minutes and replace the same volume of the dissolution medium which has been maintained at the same temperature.

7 The withdrawn samples are filtered through a whatmann filter paper and measure the absorbance at 276 nm and calculate the concentration of the tetracycline HCl dissolved at each time interval

8 Run at least two experiments so that the results are satisfactorily reproducible

9 Compare the results for the data obtained for the tetyracycline HCl dissolved with antacid and without antacid.

Observation table: Table I (Without antacid)

S.NO	Time (minutes)	Absorbance	Concentration	%age released
1	5			
2	10			
3	15			
4	20			
5	25			
6	30			
7	35			
8	40			
9	45			
10	55			
11	60			

Table II (With 0.2 % antacid)

S.NO	Time (minutes)	Absorbance	Concentration	%agereleased
1	5			
2	10			
3	15			
4	20			
5	25			
6	30			
7	35			
8	40			
9	45			
10	55			
11	60			

Result:- It was observed from the above experiment that the dissolution of the tetracycline decreased in the presence of antacid(0.2%w/v) hence the antacids markedly reduce the dissolution rate of the tetracycline from the capsules.

AIM NO.8

Apply method of residuals on the given data of drug obeying ICBM kinetics after administration as a single dose and also calculate various parameters using semilog graph paper

References: 1) Laboratory manual of biopharmaceutics and pharmacokinetics by Dr. S. B. Bise, Dr. R.J. Dias, Dr. S. C. Dhawale, Shri K.K. Mali, Trinity publishing House, Page no. 125-128

2) Biopharmaceutics and pharmacokinetics. A treatise by D. M. Brahmankar and Sunil B. Jaiswal; 278-280 vallabh parkashan, 2009

Requirements:- semilog graph paper, pencil, scale, eraser, calculator, given pharmacokinetic data

Theory:- The method of residuals can be used to calculate the absorption rate constant. This technique is also known as feathering, peeling and stripping. It is commonly used in pharmacokinetics to resolve a multiexponential curve into its individual components. For a drug that follows one –compartment kinetics and administered orally (extravascularly), the concentration of drug in plasma is expressed by a biexponential equation as:-

$$C = \frac{K_a F X_0}{V_d (k_a - k_E)} (e^{-k_e t} - e^{-k_a t}) \quad \ldots\ldots..1)$$

If $k_a F X_0 / V_d (k_a - k_E) = A$, a hybrid constant then

$$C = A e^{-k_e t} - A e^{-k_a t} \ldots\ldots..2)$$

During the elimination phase, when absorption is almost over, $k_a \gg k_E$ and the value of second exponential $e^{-k_a t}$ approaches zero whereas the first exponential $e^{-k_e t}$ retains some finite value. At this time, the equation 2 becomes as:-

$$\overleftarrow{C} = A e^{-k_e t} \ldots..3)$$

Converting the equation 3 into log form gives:-

$$\log C' = \log A - \frac{k_E t}{2.303} \quad \ldots\ldots\ldots 4)$$

Where C' represents the back extrapolated plasma concentration values. A plot of log C verses t yields a biexponential curve with a terminal linear phase having a slope $-k_E/2.303$. Back extrapolation of this straight line to time zero yields y-intercept equal to log A.

Subtraction of true plasma concentration value eq 2 from the extrapolated plasma concentration values eq 3 yields a series of residual concentrations values C_r

$$C' - C = C_r = A\, e^{-k_a t} \quad \ldots\ldots 5)$$

In log form, the eq 5 can be written as

$$\log C_r = \log A - \frac{k_a t}{2.303} \quad \ldots\ldots 6)$$

Thus a plot of log C_r versus t yields a straight line with slope $-K_a/2.303$ and y-intercept log A. Absorption half life can then be computed from Ka using the relation 0.693/Ka. Thus the method of residuals enables resolution of the biexponential plasma level – time curve into its two exponential components. The technique works best when the difference between Ka and KE is large (ka/Ke $\geq$3).

Ideally, the extrapolated and the residual lines interact each other on y-axis i.e. at time t = zero and there is no lag absorption. If an intersection occurs at a time greater than zero, it indicates time lag. The method is best suited for drugs which are rapidly and completely absorbed and follows one compartment kinetics. When using method of residuals, a minimum of three points should be used to define the straight line. Data points occurring shortly after t max may not be accurate, because drug absorption is still continuing at that time. Because this portion of the curve represents the post absorption phase, only data points from the elimination phase should be used to define the rate of drug absorption as a first order process.

Given data:- Using the following data, compute various pharmacokinetic parameters using method of residuals

Table I : The following data were obtained when a 500 mg of an antibiotic was given orally. Assume 100% of the administered dose is absorbed. Plasma data obtained after oral administration of 500mg dose of drug:-

Time (hrs)	1	2	3	4	5	6	8	16	18	20
Conc.(µg/ml)	26.501	36.091	37.512	36.055	32.924	29.413	22.784	7.57	5.734	4.343

Procedure:

1 Take a semi log graph paper and plot the drug concentration c versus time with the concentration values on logarithmic axis.

2 Then extrapolate the elimination phase of the curve obtained back upto y-axis.

3 Denote the concentrations from extrapolated line as c←.

4 Obtain c← concentrations for time ($t_1, t_2, \ldots t_n$) versus concentration ($C_1, C_2, \ldots C_n$) from back extrapolated concentrations line i.e. C_1←, C_2←,…… C_n←.

5 Obtain the residual concentrations (C_r) by subtracting C from C← with respect to time.

6 Plot a graph between the obtained residual concentrations (C_r) values and time on the semilog graph paper.

7 Determine the slope of the residual line using the formula:

Slope = log C_2← -log C_1←/t_2- t_1

8 Calculate the absorption rate constant by using slope of residual line

K_a = - slope x 2.303

9 Calculate the absorption half life ($t_{1/2}$)

$t_{1/2}$ = 0.693/ K_a

10 Also calculate the slope of the line of elimination phase and then calculate the elimination rate constant using formula:

$K_E = -\text{slope} \times 2.303$

Calculation table: Estimation of residual concentrations

Time (hr)	Plasma conc.(µg/ml)	Extrapolated concentration $C_{\leftarrow}$ (µg/ml)	Residual concentration $C_r = C_{\leftarrow} - C$ (µg/ml)
1	26.501	60	33.49
2	36.091	52	15.909
3	37.512	45	7.488
4	36.055	39	2.945
5	32.924	34	1.076
6	29.413		
8	22.784		
16	7.571		
18	5.734		
20	4.343		

AIM NO. 9

Apply method of residuals on the given plasma drug concentration –time data of a drug obeying 2CBM kinetics after IV bolus administration and calculate various PK parameters viz. intercept, microconstants and transfer rate constant using semi log graph paper

Reference: 1) Biopharmaceutics and pharmacokinetics A treatise by D.M.Brahmankar and S.B.Jaiswal, page no. 292-297, vallabh parkashan, 2009.

2) Fundamentals of biopharmaceutics and pharmacokinetics by V Venketswarlu, Paras publishing, page no.193-196

Requirements: Semilog graph paper, pencil, scale, eraser, calculator, given data

Theory: The commonest of all multicompartment models is a two compartment model. In such a model, the body tissues are broadly classified into 2 categories:-

1) Central compartment or compartment 1 comprising of blood and highly perfused tissues like liver, lungs, kidneys etc that equilibrate with the drug rapidly. Elimination occurs from this compartment

2) Peripheral or tissue compartment or compartment 2 comprising of poorly perfused and slow equilibrating tissues such as muscles, skin, adipose etc and considered as a hybrid of several functional physiological units.

As the i.v. bolus of a drug that follows two compartment kinetics, the decline in plasma concentration is biexponential indicating the presence of two dissolution processes viz. distribution and elimination. These two processes are not evident to the eyes in a regular arithmatic plot but when a semilog plot of C versus t is made, they can be identified. Initially, the concentration of drug in the central compartment declines rapidly, this is due to the distribution of drug from the central compartment to the peripheral compartment. The phase during which this occurs is called as the distribution phase. The second, slower rate process is called as the post – distribution or elimination phase. In contrast to the central compartment, the drug concentration in the peripheral compartment first increases and reaches a maximum. This corresponds with the distribution phase. Following peak, the drug declines which corresponds to the post distribution phase.

Let K_{12} and K_{21} be the first order distribution rate constants depicting drug transfer between the central and the peripheral compartments and let subscript c and p define the central and peripheral compartment respectively. The rate of change in drug concentration in the central compartment is given by

$$\frac{dC_c}{dt} = K_{21}C_p - K_{12}C_c - K_E C_c \quad \ldots\ldots 1$$

Extending the relationship $X = V_d C$ to the above equation, we have

$$\frac{dC_c}{dt} = \frac{K_{21} X_p}{V_p} - \frac{K_{12} X_c}{V_c} - \frac{K_E X_c}{V_c} \quad \ldots\ldots 2)$$

Where X_c and X_p are the amounts of drug in the central and peripheral compartments respectively and V_C and V_p are the apparent volumes of the central and the peripheral compartment respectively. The rate of change in drug concentration in the peripheral compartment is given by :-

$$\frac{dC_p}{dt} = K_{12}C_C - K_{21}C_P \quad \ldots\ldots 3)$$

$$= \frac{K_{12}X_C}{V_C} - \frac{K_{21}X_P}{V_p} \quad \ldots\ldots 4)$$

Integrating the equations 3 and 4 yield the equations that describe the concentration of drug in the central and peripheral compartments at any given time t :-

$$C_c = \frac{X_0}{V_C}\left[\frac{(K_{21}-\alpha)}{\beta-\alpha} e^{-\alpha t} + \frac{(K_{21}-\beta)}{\alpha-\beta} e^{-\beta t}\right] \quad \ldots\ldots 5)$$

$$C_p = \frac{X_0}{V_p}\left[\frac{(K_{12})}{\beta-\alpha} e^{-\alpha t} + \frac{(K_{12})}{\alpha-\beta} e^{-\beta t}\right] \quad \ldots\ldots 6)$$

Where X_0 = i.v. bolus dose, α and β are the hybrid first order constants for the rapid distribution phase and the slow elimination phase respectively which depend entirely upon the first order rate constants K_{12}, K_{21} and K_E

The constants K_{12} and K_{21} that depict reversible transfer of drug between compartments are called as microconstants or transfer constants.

The mathematical relationships between hybrid and microconstants are given as:-

$\alpha + \beta = K_{12} + K_{21} + K_E$ ....7)

$\alpha\beta = K_{21}K_E$ ....8)

Equation 5) can be written in simplified form as:-

$C_c = Ae^{-\alpha t} + Be^{-\beta t}$

Where C_c = distribution exponent + elimination exponent

A and B are also hybrid constants for the two exponents and be resolved graphically by the method of residuals.

$$A = \frac{X_0 [k_{21} - \alpha]}{V_c \, \beta - \alpha} = \frac{C_0 [k_{21} - \alpha]}{\beta - \alpha} \ldots\ldots 9)$$

$$B = \frac{X_0 [k_{21} - \beta]}{V_c \, \alpha - \beta} = \frac{C_0 [k_{21} - \beta]}{\alpha - \beta} \ldots\ldots 10)$$

where C_0 = plasma drug concentration immediately after i.v. injection

<u>Method of residuals</u> : The biexponential disposition curve obtained after i.v. bolus of a drug that fits two compartment model can be resolved into its individual exponents by the method of residuals.

From the following equation:

$C_c = Ae^{-\alpha t} + Be^{-\beta t}$

As apparent from the biexponential curve, the initial decline due to distribution is more rapid than the terminal decline due to elimination i.e. the rate constant $\alpha \gg \beta$ and hence the term $e^{-\alpha t}$ approaches zero much faster than does $e^{-\beta t}$. Thus the equation 11) reduced to

$C \leftarrow = Be^{-\beta t}$ ....12)

Converting the equation 12) into log form

$$\log C_{\leftarrow} = \log B - \frac{\beta t}{2.303} \quad \ldots\ldots 13)$$

Where $C_{\leftarrow}$ = back extrapolated plasma concentration values.

A semilog plot of C versus t yield the terminal linear phase of the curve having slope $-\beta/2.303$ and when back extrapolated to time zero, yields y-intercept log B. The $t_{1/2}$ for the α

$$C_r = C - C_{\leftarrow} = Ae^{-\alpha t} \quad \ldots\ldots 14)$$

Converting this equation into log form gives:-

$$\log C_r = \log A - \frac{\alpha t}{2.303}$$

A semilog plot of C_r versus t yields a straight line with slope $-\alpha/2.303$ and y intercept log A

Given data: A dose of 100mg of drug is administered by rapid i.v injection to a 70 kg healthy adult male. Blood samples are taken periodically after the administration of the drug and plasma fraction of each sample of the drug is assayed. The following data is obtained:-Assume the drug follows 2CBM, Calculate all the PK parameters.

Procedure:-

1 Take a semilog graph paper and plot a graph of plasma concentration versus t.

2 Calculate the slope of the terminal linear portion of the graph

3 Calculate the elimination rate constant β from the slope using the formula slope = $-\frac{\beta}{2.303}$

(hr^{-1}) β = -slope x 2.303

4 Calculate the elimination half life using the formula

$= 0.693/\beta$ hrs

5 Extrapolate the terminal linear portion of the graph to cut on y-axis and find the y intercept

Intercept $B = \dfrac{X_0(k_{21}-\beta)}{V_c(\alpha-\beta)} = \ldots\ldots \mu g/ml$

6 Apply method of residuals and set up the table i.e. obtain Concentrations for time $(t_1, t_2, \ldots t_n)$ vs concentration $(C_1, C_2, \ldots C_n)$ from back extrapolated line i.e. $C_1\leftarrow, C_2\leftarrow \ldots\ldots C_n\leftarrow$.

7 Obtain the residual concentrations (C_r) by subtracting C from C← with respect to time and set up the table as given below.

Time	Observed concentration	Extrapolated C←values	Residual concentration(C_r= C-C←)
0.25	43		
0.5	32		
1.0	20		
1.5	14		
2.0	11		
4.0	6.5		
8.0	2.8		
12.0	1.2		
16.0	0.52		

8. Plot a graph between the obtained residual concentrations (C_r) values vs time on the same graph paper to obtain a residual line, calculate the slope of this line and intercept A.

9. Calculate α from the slope

As slope = $-\alpha/2.303$

α = -slope x 2.303 hr^{-1}

Intercept A=……..μg/ml

10. Now, the equation becomes

$$C= Ae^{-\alpha t}+ Be^{-\beta t}$$

11. Calculate the other rate constants as following

$$K_{21}= \frac{B\alpha + AB}{A+B} = …….hr^{-1}$$

$$K_{13} = \frac{(A+B)\, \alpha\beta}{B\alpha+A\beta} =…….. hr^{-1}$$

$$K_{12} = \frac{AB(\alpha-\beta)^2}{(A+B)(B\alpha+A\beta)}=…….. hr^{-1}$$

12. Calculate volume of distribution of the central compartment (V_c) as

$$A+B = C_0= \frac{X_0}{V_c}$$

V_c(in mililitres)= $\frac{X_0}{C_0}$ = $\frac{I.V.dose}{A+B}$ = $\frac{100mg}{…..μg/ml+….. μg/ml}$

13. Calculate the area under curve from 0 –infinity using trapezoidal rule

$$AUC_t^{infinity} = \frac{C^*}{\beta}$$

Where β = slope of the terminal phase

14. Calculate the concentration of drug in tissue or peripheral compartment as:-

$$X_t = \frac{K_{12} X_0 (e^{-\beta t} - e^{-\alpha t})}{(\alpha - \beta)}$$

Eg:- the amount of drug in tissues compartment after i.v. bolus injection is estimated using the equation:-

$$X_t = \frac{0.78 \times 100 (e^{-0.21 \times 4} - e^{-1.8 \times 4})}{(1.8 - 0.21)}$$

$= 49.06(0.431) = 21.16$ mg

15. Calculate the amount of drug in the central compartment after 4 hrs $X_c = V_C \cdot C$

i.e. $V_C \times 6.5$ mg/ml = ...mg

16. Calculate the total amount of drug in the body after 4 hrs = $X_c + X_t$ = ...mg

17. Calculate volume at steady state V_d^{ss}

$$V_d^{ss} = \frac{\text{Total drug in body at steady state}}{\text{Plasma drug concentration}}$$

$$= \frac{X_c + X_t}{6.5 \mu g/ml} = \ldots\ldots L$$

18. Calculate V_d^{exp}

$$V_d^{exp} = \frac{V_c (\alpha - \beta)}{(k_{21} - \beta)}$$

AIM NO.10

To compute various pharmacokinetic parameters from the given plasma drug concentration –time data of first order process using semilog graph paper and write down the equation for the line produced on the graph

Reference:- 1) Biopharmaceutics and pharmacokinetics A treatise by D.M.Brahmankar and Sunil B. Jaiswal; page no 242-243, vallabh parkashan,2009

2) Biopharmaceutics & pharmacokinetics (Theoretical concepts & Illustrative practical exercises) by Dr. Javed Ali, Dr. Alka Ahuja, Dr. Sanjula Baboota and Dr. Roop K.Khar

Requirements:- Semi log graph paper, pencil, ruler, calculator, eraser, given pharmacokinetic data

Theory: A first order process is the one whose rate is directly proportional to the concentration of drug undergoing reaction i.e. greater the concentration, faster is the reaction. A first order process is also called as the process following linear kinetics. According to the first order kinetics, the rate of reaction of a drug can be written as:-

$$\frac{dC}{dt} = -KC \quad \ldots\ldots..1)$$

Where K = first order rate constant (in time^{-1})

dC/dt = Rate of reaction

and C = concentration of drug at given time t

Rearranging the equation 1 gives

$$\frac{dC}{C} = -Kdt \quad \ldots\ldots.2)$$

Integrating the equation 2 gives

$$\ln C = \ln C_0 - kt \quad \ldots..3)$$

In exponential form, equation 3 can be written as

$C = C_0 e^{-kt}$ ……4)

Where e = natural log phase

As the equation 4 has only one exponent, the first order process is also called as monoexponential rate process. Thus a first order process is charaterized by logarithmic or exponential kinetics i.e. a constant fraction of drug undergoes reaction per unit time.

Converting the equation 3 into log form gives

$\log C = \log C_0 - \dfrac{kt}{2.303}$ ……5)

Sbstituting the value of $C = C_0/2$ at $t_{1/2}$ in equation 5 gives

$t_{1/2} = 0.693/k$ ……6)

Procedure: Using the following intravenous pharmacokinetic data, calculate the various pharmacokinetic parameters

Data:- i.v. administration of 37.5mg of drug

Time (hrs)	Plasma concentration (mg/ml)
0.8	11.6
2	11.2
4	10.38
5	10.32
7	10.13
10	10.04

1. Take a semilog graph paper and plot the above data taking the plasma concentration on y-axis and time on x-axis

2. Find the slope of the line obtained using the equation

$$\text{Slope} = \frac{\log C_1 - \log C_2}{t_1 - t_2}$$

3. Calculate the elimination rate constant K_e using the equation:-

$K_e = -2.303 \times \text{slope}$

4. Calculate the $t_{1/2}$ using the formula:-

$t_{1/2} = 0.693 / K_e$

5. Calculate the apparent volume of distribution (V_d):-

$V_d = \text{dose}/C_0$

Where C_0 = concentration at time 0, calculated from the intercept after extrapolation as according to following equation

$$\log C = \log C_0 - \frac{kt}{2.303}$$

Intercept = $\log C_0$

6. Calculate clearance using the equation

Clearance = $V_d \times K_e$

7. Calculate $AUC_{0-\infty}$ using the following formula:-

$AUC_{0-\infty} = C_0 / K_e$

7. calculate $AUC_{t-\infty}$ using the formula:-

$AUC_{t-\infty} = C_t / K_e$

8. Calculate $AUC_{0-infinity}$ using the equation:

$AUC_{0-infinity} = AUC_{0-t} + AUC_{t-infinity}$

9. Write the equation for the line produced on graph:-

$$\log C = \log C_0 - \frac{k_e t}{2.303}$$

Results:- The various pharmacokinetic parameters of the given data are:-

1) The value of elimination rate constant K_e is found to be ....

2) The value of $t_{1/2}$ is found to be ....

3) The value of V_d is found to be ....

4) The value of clearance C_L is found to be ....

5) AUC_{0-t} is found to be ....

6) $AUC_{t-infinity}$ is found to be ....

7) $AUC_{0-infinity}$ is found to be ....

AIM NO.11

To determine the absolute bioavailability and relative bioavailability from the given plasma concentration time data of the formulations containing the same drug

Reference:-

1) Biopharmaceutics & pharmacokinetics by Dr. Javed Ali, Dr. Alka ahuja, Dr. Sanjula Baboota, Dr. Roop k.khar, Page no 324-326

2) Biopharmaceutics and pharmacokinetics A tretise by D.H.Brahmankar and Sunil B. Jaiswal

Requirements: Regular graph paper, pencil, calculator

Theory: Bioavailability is defined as the rate and extent of drug absorption in systemic circulation. In other words, it is the fraction of an administered dose that actually reaches the systemic circulation.

Absolute bioavailability:- The absolute bioavailability of a drug product may be measured by comparing respective AUCs after oral and i.v. administration of the same dose of same drugs. Absolute bioavailability using plasma data can be determined as follows:-

$$\text{Absolute bioavailability} = \frac{AUC_{p.o} \times dose_{i.v}}{AUC_{i.v.} \times dose_{p.o.}}$$

Where p.o. stands for per oral

The absolute bioavailability is equal to 'F' the fraction of the dose is bioavailable. For drugs given vascularly such as by i.v. bolus injection F=1, since all the drug is completely bioavailable. For all extra vascular routes of administration, $F \leq 1$

Relative bioavailability: Relative (apparent bioavailability) is the bioavailability of a drug product as compared to a recognized standard formulation. It is compared to the bioavailability of drug in a standard dosage formulation usually a solution of the free drug. The relative bioavailability of two drug products given at the same dosage level and by the same route of administration can be obtained by the following equation:-

$$\text{Relative bioavailability (\%)} = \frac{[AUC]_A}{[AUC]_B} \times 100$$

Where drug product B is recognized as reference standard. This fraction may be multiplied by 100 to give % relative bioavailability

Methods of assessing bioavailability:- There are several direct and indirect methods of assessing bioavailability. The selection of method depends on:-

A purpose of the study

B The analytical method of drug measurement

C The nature of the drug product

Methods to assess bioavailability :-(Indirect methods)

(A) plasma data

1 The time of peak plasma blood concentration(t_{max})

2 The peak plasma concentration (C_{max})

3 The area under the plasma level – time curve (AUC)

Plasma data:- The plasma drug concentration time curve (blood level curve) is the focal point of bioavailability assessment and is obtained when serial samples are taken after drug administration and analyzed for drug concentration. This is the method of choice.

(a) t_{max}: It is the time required to reach maximum drug concentration after drug administration. At t_{max}, absorption is maximized. The rate of drug absorption equals the rate of drug elimination. It can be used as an approximate indication of drug absorption rate.

(b) C_{max}:-The peak plasma concentration represents the maximum plasma drug concentration obtained after oral administration of drug. It provides an indication that the drug is sufficiently systemically absorbed to provide a therapeutic response.

(c) AUC: The area under the plasma level time curve is a measurement of the extent of bioavailability of a drug. It reflects the total amount of active drug that reaches the systemic circulation. The AUC is the area under the drug plasma level time curve from time zero to infinity and is equal to amount of unchanged drug reaching the general circulation divided by the clearance.

(B) Urine data:

1 The cumulative amount of drug excreted in the urine (D_u)

2 The rate of drug excreation in the urine (dD_u/dt)

3 The time for maximum urinary excreation(t_a)

This method is successful provided that the active ingredient is excreted unchanged in a significant quantity in the urine and complete samples of curve must be collected.

1) D_u: It is related to AUC of the plasma level data and increases as the extent of absorption increases.

2) dD_u/dt: It is analogous to C_{max} and is obtained from the peak of plot between rate of excreation versus midpoint time of urine collection period. Its value increases as rate/absorption extent increases.

3) T_a: The time for maximum excretion rate is analogous to the t_{max} of plasma level data. Its value decreases as the rate of absorption increases.

Procedure:

Given data:

Time (hrs)	Plasma concentration(µg/ml) (i.v.)	Plasma concentration (µg/ml) (oral)
0.5	6.82	0.97
1	4.47	3.46
1.5	3.14	4.02
2	2.21	3.32
3	1.15	1.62
4	0.55	0.85
5	0.28	0.39
6	0.14	0.19
7	0.07	0.09

Using the following data of the different formulations containing the same drug, calculate the absolute bioavailability

1) Using weigh and cut method:- Take two regular graph paper and then plot the graph between the plasma concentration (on y-axis) and time on x-axis for the data of each formulation

a) Extrapolate the graphs to zero and then cut the graph and weigh them individually. Use the following formula to calculate absolute bioavailability:-

Absolute bioavailability = weight of oral x 100

Weight of i.v.

2 Area method:- In this method, the squares under the curve are counted. Squares having area more than half in the graph are also counted. Calculate the absolute bioavailability using the formula:-

$$\text{Absolute bioavailability} = \frac{\text{Area of oral}}{\text{Area of i.v.}} \times 100$$

2) Trapezoidal method:- This is the most accurate method to obtain bioavailability. It involves the breaking up of the plasma concentration versus time profile into several trapezoids. Calculate the areas of individual trapezoids and then add up these areas to arrive at a cumulative AUC.

$$\text{Area under curve trapezoid} = \frac{1}{2} (c_1 + c_2)(t_2 - t_1)$$

$$\text{Absolute bioavailability} = \frac{AUC_{oral}}{AUC_{i.v.}} \times 100$$

Result: The absolute and relative bioavailability of formulations containing the same drug was found to be ………. and ………respectively

AIM NO.12

To compute various PK parameters using non-compartmental analysis from orally administered drug data

References:- 1) PHAR7633 chapter 20, non compartmental analysis (http://www.boomer org/c/p4/c20/C20.html)

2) Biopharmaceutics and pharmacokinetics A treatise by D.H. Brahmankar and Sunil B. Jaiswal, Vallabh prakashan, edition 2009, page no. 254-255

Requirements: Regular graph paper, pencil, scale, eraser, calculator

Theory: The non-compartmental analysis is also known as the model independent method does not require the assumption of specific compartmental model. It is based on the assumption that the drugs or metabolites follow linear kinetics and this technique can be applied on any compartmental model. The non compartmental approach is based on the statistical moments theory, involves collection of experimental data following a single dose of drug. If one considers the time course of drug concentration in plasma as a statistical distribution curve, then

$$MRT = \frac{AUMC}{AUC}$$

Where MRT = mean residence time

AUMC = area under the first moment curve

AUC = area under the zero moment curve

AUMC is obtained from a plot of product of plasma concentration and time (i.e. c.t) versus time t from zero to infinity

It is expressed by equation:-

$$AUMC = \int_0^{\infty} c\,t\,dt \quad \ldots\ldots..1)$$

AUC is obtained from a plot of plasma drug concentration versus time from zero to infinity.

Mathematically, it can be expressed by equation:-

$$AUC = {_0\int^{infinity}} c \, dt \ldots\ldots 2)$$

Practically the AUC and AUMC can be calculated from the respective graphs by the trapezoidal rule. MRT is defined as the average amount of time spent by the drug in the body before elimination. It is the statistical analogy of half life, $t_{1/2}$. MRT represents the time for 63.2% of the i.v.bolus dose to be eliminated.

Applications of non-compartmental method are:-

1) It is widely used to estimate the important parameters like bioavailability, clearance and apparent volume of distribution

2) The method is useful in determining half-life, rate of absorption and first-order absorption rate constant for the drug

As AUC is given by equation

$$AUC = {_0\int^{infinity}} t^0 \times c_p \times dt = {_0\int^{infinity}} c_p \times dt \ldots\ldots 3)$$

$$AUMC = {_0\int^{infinity}} t^0 \times c_p \times dt \ldots\ldots 4)$$

Cl_T (Total systemic clearance, v_{ss}, the volume of distribution at steady state, v_d, MRT are calculated from AUC and AUMC using following equations:-

$$Cl = \frac{dose}{AUC} \ldots\ldots 5)$$

$$MRT = \frac{AUMC}{AUC} \ldots\ldots 6)$$

$$V_{ss} = \frac{dose \times AUMC}{AUC^2} = cl \times MRT \ldots\ldots 7)$$

For an accurate calculation of the different PK parameters, the AUC and AUMC from time zero to infinity are required.

The extrapolation from the time of the last measured concentration (t_{last}) is done by mathematical integration of the curve from t_{last} to infinity

$$AUC_{extrapolated} = \frac{C(last)}{\lambda} \quad \ldots\ldots 8)$$

Where c (last) = last measured concentration

λ = slope of the terminal phase

Similarly $AUMC_{extrapolated} = \frac{t_{last} \times C(t_{last})}{\lambda} + \frac{C(t_{last})}{\lambda^2} \quad \ldots\ldots 9)$

Total $AUC = AUC_{0-tlast} + \frac{C_{p\,last}}{\lambda} \quad \ldots\ldots 10)$

$$F = \frac{AUC_{p.o.} \times Dose_{i.v.}}{AUC_{i.v.} \times dose_{p.o}} \quad \ldots\ldots 11)$$

As $cl = \frac{dx/dt}{C_p} = \frac{\text{Rate of elimination}}{C_p}$

$cl.C_p = dx/dt$ Rearrange & integrate

$cl.\int C_p.dt = \int dy$

$cl.\,AUC = X\,(dose)$

$cl = \frac{dose}{AUC}$ for i.v. and $cl = \frac{F\,dose}{AUC}$ for e.v. $\ldots\ldots 12)$

$AUMC = AUMC_{0-t(last)} + \frac{C_{p\,last}.t_{last}}{\lambda} + \frac{C_{last}}{\lambda^2} \quad \ldots\ldots 13)$

where λ is slope of terminal phase

MRT = AUMC/AUC......14)

Apparent elimination constant K_E = 1/MRT .....15) for an i.v. dose of drug

V_{ss} = MRT.Cl......16)

As $cl_T = K_E V_d$........17)

$V_d = cl / K_E$ = dose/k_EAUC for i.v. ....18)

$V_d = FX_0 / K_E AUC$ for e.v. ....19)

Additional parameters which can be calculated are

MAT = $MRT_{p.o.}$ - $MRT_{i.v.}$ ....20)

K_a = apparent absorption rate

Given data:- plasma concentration – time data after oral administration of 250 mg of drug is :-

Time (hrs)	Plasma concentration(mg/lt)
0	0
1	12.18
2	14.12
3	13.43
4	12.16
6	9.64
9	6.73
12	4.69
18	2.28
24	1.11
Infinity	

Procedure :

1) Take a regular graph paper and plot the given data of plasma concentration versus time profile

2) Divide the graph into a series of vertical lines to prepare segments(trapezoids)

3) Calculate the area of each segment using formula:

$$AUC = \frac{(t_n - t_{n-1})(C_{n-1} + C_n)}{2}$$

4) Then sum the area of all trapezoids to yield AUC from time zero to infinity

5) The AUC $_{last-infinity}$ is calculated by equation:

$$AUC_{last-infinity} = \frac{\text{last plasma concentration}}{\lambda}$$

Where λ = slope of the terminal phase

6) Similarly find AUMC of each segment using formula:

$$AUMC = \frac{(C_{n-1} + C_n) \times t_n(t_n - t_{n-1})}{2}$$

7) Find $AUMC_{last-infinity} = \frac{C_{P\,last} \times t_{last}}{\lambda} + \frac{C_{P\,last}}{\lambda^2}$

8) Similarly sum all the AUMC of all trapezoids from the zero to infinity to get the total AUMC value

9) Then calculate MRT(in hours) using the following equation

$$MRT = AUC/AUMC$$

10) Then calculate apparent K_E(elimination rate constant) using the equation:

$$K_E = 1/MRT \text{ (units hr}^{-1}\text{)}$$

11) Then calculate V_{SS} by formula:

$$V_{SS} = MRT \cdot CL \text{ (in litres)}$$

12) Then calculate v_d using the formula:

$$v_d = Cl/K_E \text{ (litres)}$$

13) Then calculate MAT

As $MAT = MRT_{poral} - MRT_{i.v.}$

As $MRT_{I.V.} = 1/\lambda$ Hence calculate MAT

14) Calculate Apparent absorption rate constant

$$K_a = 1/MAT$$

www.ingramcontent.com/pod-product-compliance
Lightning Source LLC
LaVergne TN
LVHW070529070526
838199LV00073B/6731